My Samsung Galaxy S21 Ultra User's Manual

A Complete User's Guide with Pro Tips and Tricks to Master Your Samsung Galaxy S21 Ultra 5G with Screenshots

Edwin Brown

Table of Contents

v

Introductory Note

Introducing the Galaxy Samsung S21 Ultra 5G smartphone features Galaxy's fastest processor with the first-ever S Pen compatibility on a Samsung Galaxy phone.

This guide is designed to help you navigate the device with ease, master its functions and get exclusive tips that will make you use the device like a pro.

Be informed that in this guide, some words are in italics; most of them are options that you will find on the device.

Basic Information/Tech Specification

Dimensions: (6.5 x 2.98 x 0.35) in

Weight: 8.01 oz.

Body Material: Aluminum frame, and Gorilla Glass Victus for front and back glass.

Display size: 6.8 inches

Display resolution: 1440 x 3200 pixel

Display type: Dynamic AMOLED 2X, 120Hz, HDR10+, 1500 nits

Front camera: 40MP (f/2.2)

Rear camera: 108MP wide (f/1.8)

Operating System (OS): Android 11, One UI 3.1

S Pen support: Yes

CPU: Snapdragon 888

Memory card slot: N/A

Internal Memory: 128GB ROM, 12GB RAM; 256GB ROM, 12GB RAM, 512GB ROM, 16GB RAM.

3.5mm jack: N/A
NFC: Yes

Battery: Non-removable Li-Ion 5000mAh

Getting Started

It's time to get started with your new Samsung Galaxy S21 Ultra 5G device. Get acquainted with the controls and functions, as well as maximizing the device potentiality. However, we need to set up the device for first-time use.

The first thing to do is charge your device battery fully before anything else.

Charging your Samsung S21 Ultra device battery

A 5000 mAh rechargeable battery powers your Samsung S21 Ultra. The device comes with a USB Type-C cable which you can use with a USB Type-C power adapter or any other device that has USB-C ports.

Pro Tips on charging safety

- Use only Samsung-approved battery, charger, and charge cable that is designed specifically for your Samsung S21 Ultra.

- In the event of charging, if you discover that your phone and charger become hot and cease charging, disconnect the charger from the phone and allow it to cool for some time before charging it again.

- If you wish to use a charger, ensure to use an approved wireless charger or an approved wire that ensures optimal charging performance.

- When using a charger, always disconnect it from the electric socket when it is not in use.

Note: Your device doesn't come with a wall charger, so you will have to purchase it separately. Visit samsung.com for more information on your device charging compatibility.

You can charge other compatible Samsung devices using your Samsung S21 Ultra device wirelessly (Read more on Wireless power sharing for more information).

Installing your SIM or USIM card

Your Samsung S21 Ultra device uses a nano-SIM card. You can use a preinstalled SIM card provided by your cellular carrier.

To install your SIM card, place the SIM into the tray. Note that when placing your SIM into the tray, the gold contact of the SIM card should be facing up.

To install your SIM or USIM card, follow the steps below:

Step I: Loosen the tray by inserting the ejection pin into the tray's hole.

Step II: As soon as the tray loosens up, gently pull out the tray from the tray slot

Step III Place your nano-SIM or USIM card on the tray and gently press it into the tray to ensure it is firmly placed.

Step IV: Insert the card tray back into the tray slot, and ensure it is closed.

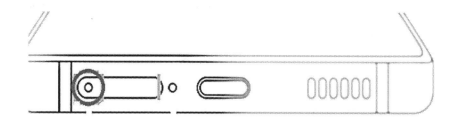

***The encircled hole is the tray's hole while the other is the Microphone's hole.

Precautions

-   If your SIM isn't a nano-SIM card, do not use it with the device.
-   Ensure your SIM tray is dry at all times.
-   Before putting the ejection pin into the tray's hole, ensure you locate it correctly, so you don't put the pin into the Microphone's hole to avoid the risk of damaging your device.

Setting Up Your Device

Now that the SIM card has been installed and the device battery is fully charged, we can set up the device for first-time use.

First, turn on the device.

Turn on/off, and restart your device

→ To **turn on** the device, press and hold the Side key

→ To **turn off** the device, press and hold the Side key and Volume down keys simultaneously, and tap Power off.

→ To **restart** the device, press and hold the Side key and Volume down keys simultaneously, tap Restart and then confirm.

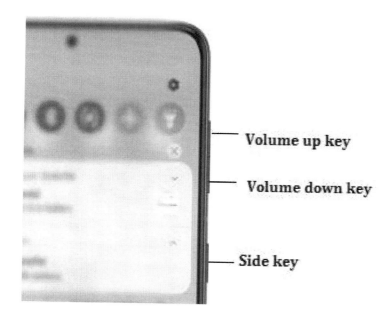

Volume up key

Volume down key

Side key

Once the device is turned on, the next step is to set up the device using the *Setup Wizard.*

Set up your device for the first time using the Setup Wizard

When you turn on your device for the first time, the Setup Wizard takes you through the basics of setting up your device. This guides you through accounts setup, choosing default languages, connect to a Wi-Fi network, as well as learning more about your device's features, and many more. You can skip some steps during setup and then address them later.

When you are done with the first-time setup, your device is ready for your use.

If you have an old device, you can transfer your data from an old device to your new Samsung S21 device. Check the next piece for more instructions.

How to transfer data to your Samsung S21 Ultra from an old device

With Smart Switch, you can transfer your files from an old device into your new device. Smart Switch works through USB cable, Wi-Fi, or computer.

Check out the procedure below:

→ Go to *Settings* > tap (Accounts and backup) > *Bring data from old device*

→ Follow the instructions and finally select the content you wish to transfer.

For more information on using Smart Switch to transfer data, click

samsung.com/us/support/owners/app/smart-switch

Mastering Your Device Basic Gesture and Status Icons: Navigate Your Screen Like A Pro

The touch screen is designed to respond best to light touches from your finger or a capacitive stylus. You don't have to exert excessive force on the touch screen.

Note: The warranty will not cover any damage caused by exerting excessive force on your touch screen. Therefore, you must handle your touch screen with great care.

Now, let's examine the basic screen touch gesture that will help you navigate your device flawlessly.

1. Tap

You can use the tap gesture to select or launch an item and use it to zoom an image in or out.

- Tap an item lightly to select it
- To zoom an image in or out, double-tap the image.

2. Touch and hold

The touch and hold gesture can be used basically in three ways:

- Display a pop-up menu of options: Touch and hold a field.
- Customize the Home screen: Touch and hold a Home screen.
- Activate an item: Touch and hold such item.

3. Swipe

To swipe, drag your finger across the screen lightly. You can swipe the screen to unlock your phone (depending on your security settings).

You can use the swipe gesture to scroll through your device Home screens or menu options.

4. Drag and drop

Before you can drag and drop an item, you need to touch and hold it before moving it to a new location. You can drag and drop an app shortcut to a Home screen as well as dragging a widget and placing it in a new location.

5. Zoom in and out

Using your thumb and forefinger together, you can zoom in and out.

- To zoom in, move your thumb and forefinger apart on the screen.
- To zoom out, move your thumb and forefinger close on the screen.

Navigation buttons

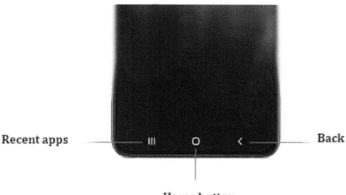

Recent apps ——— III   O   ‹ ——— Back

Home button

The navigation buttons beneath your phone's screen can be used to navigate your device quickly. You can modify the display for your navigation buttons by changing which side of the screen the Recent apps icon and Back button display. (In other words, Recent apps icon can be switched to the right, while the Back button goes to the left).

Here's how:

→ Go to *Settings* > tap ⚙ (Display) > *Navigation bar* > *Buttons*

→ Under the Button order, tap an option to choose the side of the screen you want your Back and Recent apps icons to be.

You can also hide the navigation buttons from the bottom of your screen. When you do this, you will have to swipe to navigate your device.

→ Go to *Settings* > tap (Display) > *Navigation bar* > *Swipe gesture*

→ Tap an option to customize from the list of options.

The Status Bar

The Status bar comprises the status icons angle (right side), and the notification icons angle (left side). The notification icons give information about the notification alerts, while the status icons provide device information.

Status icons	Description
	The battery is fully charged
	Battery is charging
	Airplane mode is activated
	Alarm
	Bluetooth active
	Location is active
	Vibrate
	Mute

Notification icons	Description
	Missed calls
	The call is in progress
	New Message
	New email
	Voicemail
	App update
	Download is in progress
	Upload is in progress

Pro Tip: You can modify the display options for the Status bar. This can be done from *Quick settings*, tap ⋮ (More options), and then the

Status bar. From the Status bar option, you can choose to do any of these:

- Show notification icons: This option allows you to modify how you want your notification icons to display on the Status bar.
- Show battery percentage: Display the battery charge level percentage right beside the battery icon.

Maximizing the Potentiality of The Side Key: Side Key Settings

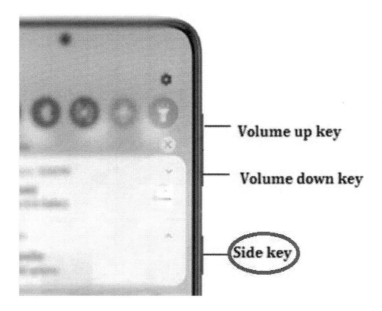

Volume up key

Volume down key

Side key

The Side key isn't only meant for locking and unlocking your device; it can also be used to launch some features. It is your responsibility to customize the shortcuts assigned to the Side key.

Side key settings

- **Press and hold the Side key shortcut**

If you want to press and hold the Side key to launch a feature, then you can choose the feature by following the path below:

→ Go to *Settings* > tap (Advanced features) > *Side key*

→ Proceed to tap *Press and hold,* and tap an option to choose which feature will be launched when you press and hold the Side key.

- **Double press the Side key**

By default, when you double press the Side key, it launches Camera. However, you can choose another feature for that command.

→ Go to *Settings* > tap (Advanced features) > *Side key*

→ Tap *Double press,* and then tap an option to choose which feature will be launched when you press the Side key twice.

Setting Up Your Account: Email, Calendar, Contacts, And More + Setting up Voicemail

You can set up and manage your accounts on your device. To use this feature, you must have an active internet connection either from your cellular provider or through a Wi-Fi network.

You can add an email account such as a Google account, Samsung account, Yahoo account, Outlook, and so on. You can also add an account that supports calendars, contacts and other compatible features.

Add a Google Account to your device

If you have an existing Google Account, you can sign in to access your Google Cloud Storage, and installed apps on your account retrieved on your new device.

Follow the procedure below:

→ Go to *Settings* > tap 🔄 (Accounts and backup) > *Manage accounts*

→ Tap ➕ (Add account) > *Google*

→ Enter your login information

*You might be required to enter your device PIN code if you have created one.

Add an Outlook account

→ Go to *Settings* > tap 🔄 (Accounts and backup) > *Manage accounts*

→ Tap ➕ (Add account) > *Outlook*

→ Enter your login information

*You might be required to enter your device PIN code if you have created one.

Add a Samsung Account to your device

If you switch from a Samsung device to another, you can sign in to your existing Samsung account to get access to exclusive Samsung content, including Samsung apps.

→ Go to *Settings* > *Samsung account*

→ Enter your login details and follow the prompt

*If you don't have an existing account, you can sign up as well here.

Set up Voicemail

When you attempt to use the voicemail service for the first time, you are prompted to set it up. This can be done using the Phone app.

Note: Options vary by carrier

→ Go to (Phone)

→ Touch and hold (1 key) or tap Voicemail.

→ Follow the prompt to create a password, and more.

Customizing Your Home Screen

Your Home screen allows you to place your favorite apps and widgets on it. Additionally, you can create more Home screens, delete screens, and reorder screens. When you have multiples Home screens, you can choose your main Home screen.

Add/remove app icons to/from the Home screen

From any of your Home screens, you can launch an app using the app icon. Before an app icon can appear on a Home screen, you need to add it to the Home screen.

How?

→ Go to Apps, locate the app you wish to add to a Home screen.

→ Touch and hold the app icon

→ Tap 🏠⊕ (Add to Home).

To remove an app icon from a Home screen;

→ Go to the Home screen, touch and hold the app icon you wish to remove.

→ Tap 🗑 (Remove).

Note: Removing an app icon from the Home screen does not mean that it is deleted from your device.

Customize your Home screen wallpaper

You can alter the look and feel of your Home and Lock screens by choosing a picture or video from your media gallery, or a preloaded wallpaper.

How?

→ On the Home screen, touch and hold any space on the screen.

→ Tap (Wallpapers); from the menus option, you can select which option you want.

Below is the description of the options:

- My wallpapers: This comprises featured and downloaded wallpapers.
- Gallery: Saved pictures and videos in the Gallery app.
- Wallpaper services: This features Dynamic Lock screen as well as additional features, including guide page.
- Apply Dark mode to Wallpaper

* You can download more wallpapers from Galaxy Themes

→ Tap a picture or video you choose to apply and tap *Done.*

***Note: Multiple pictures and videos can only be applied to the Lock screen.

→ Tap either *Set on Home screen*, *Set on Lock screen*, or *Set on Lock and Home screens*

Applying a theme

You can set your device theme which can be applied to your Home and Lock screens, as well as wallpapers and app icons.

→ Go to a Home screen, touch and hold the screen.

→ Tap ⊤ (Themes); tap a theme to preview and download it.

→ To see downloaded themes, tap ☰ (Navigation drawer) > *My stuff*

→ Tap a theme, and to apply it; tap *Apply*.

Change default icons

You can apply different icon sets in place of the original icons.

→ Go to a Home screen, touch and hold the screen.

→ Tap ▼ (Themes) > *Icons*; tap an icon set from the list to preview and download it.

→ To see downloaded icons, tap ☰ (Navigation drawer) > *My stuff* > *Icons*.

→ Tap an icon, and to apply it; tap *Apply*.

Adding Widgets to your Home screens

Adding widgets to your home screens grants you quick access to apps and certain info. Aside from that, widgets help you keep an organized home screen. You can group specific apps, and add them to a widget; hence it makes finding an app much easier.

Let's add a widget to the Home screen:

→ Go to a Home screen, touch and hold the screen.

→ Tap ⚫⚫ (Widgets); tap a widget set

→ Swipe through the widget until you find the one you want; tap *Add* to add it to the Home screen.

Manage and customize your widget

As soon as you add a widget to a home screen, you can adjust its location on the screen and how it functions.

From a Home screen, touch and hold a widget, an options menu will pop-up from which you can tap an option

- 🗑 (Remove): Choose this option to remove a widget from your screen.

- ⚙ (Settings): This option allows you to customize your widgets functions or appearance.

- ⓘ (Info): View information about widget permission and usage.

Always On Display (AOD)

Always On Display (AOD) gives you the privilege to check your device's time and date, message alert, and customized information without unlocking it.

→ To enable AOD, go to *Settings*, tap (Lock screen), and then tap *Always On Display*; then enable the feature by tapping .

After enabling the feature, you can set the following options:

- You can choose when to show a clock and notifications on the screen when your device is idle

- Clock style: This option allows you to modify the clock's style and color on the Lock screen and AOD.

- Show music information: When you use Face Widget music controller, this option shows the music details.

- Auto brightness: Automatically adjust screen brightness on AOD.

- Screen orientation: Choose portrait or landscape mode.

- About Always On Display: Show the license details and current version of the software.

Applying AOD themes

You can apply custom themes for AOD to give it a stylish display.

→ From any of the Home screen, touch and hold the screen

→ Tap (Themes), and then tap *AODs*.

→ Tap an AOD theme to preview and download it to *My Always On Displays*

→ To see downloaded themes, Tap (Navigation drawer) > *My Stuff* > *AODs*

→ Tap one of the downloaded AOD themes, and then tap *Apply*.

General Home screen settings

You can customize how you want your Home and Apps screens to be from the Home screen settings. Go to a Home screen, and then touch and hold the screen to reveal the ⚙ Settings icon. Tap ⚙ Settings to reveal the settings options, as shown below:

- *Home screen grid*: From here, you can select how you want your apps icons to be arranged on the screen (layout).

- *Home screen layout*: You can set your phone to have different Home and Apps screens, or a Home screen only with all apps located in it.

- *Apps screen grid*: Select a layout for how the icons will appear on the Apps screen.

- *Show Apps screen button on Home screen*: Choose this option to add a button to the Home screen to foster easy access to the Apps screen.

- *Add new apps to Home screen*: This makes newly downloaded apps to be added to the Home screen automatically.

- *Lock Home screen layout*: This locks the items on the Home screen from being displaced or removed.

- *Hide apps*: Hidden apps will not show in the Home and App screens. It doesn't mean they are uninstalled from your device. You can return to this path to return them to the screens.

- *App icon badges*: When you enable this, a badge shows on apps with active notifications.

- *Swipe down for notification panel*: Enabling this option will allow you to open the Notification panel by swiping down anywhere on the Home screen.

- *Rotate to landscape mode*: This makes your Home screen change to landscape orientation when you tilt your device from portrait to landscape.

- *About Home screen*: View information about the version.

The Notification panel/Quick settings

The Notification panel gives you quick access to settings and notifications.

How to view the Notification panel

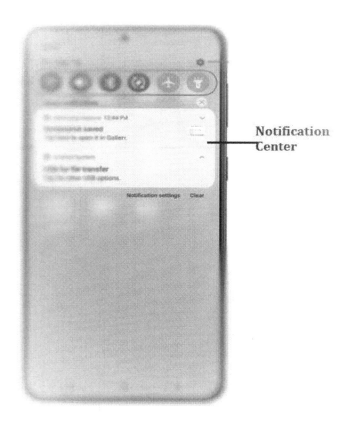

Notification Center

From any screen, you can access the Notification panel by swiping down on the screen. When you open the Notification panel, tap an item to open it. You can clear a notification from the notification screen by dragging it to the right or left; however, if you want to clear all notifications, tap *Clear*. Tap *Notification settings* to customize notifications.

To close the Notification panel, tap ⟨ (Back) or drag upward from the screen's bottom.

Quick settings

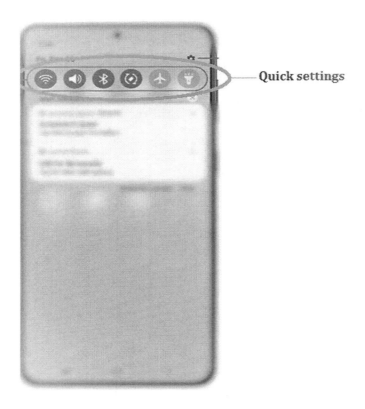

Quick settings

The Notification panel also gives quick access to Quick settings. You can turn on/off features like Wi-Fi, Bluetooth, Airplane mode, flashlight, and more from Quick settings.

To reveal the Quick setting, swipe down with two fingers from the top of the screen.

Below are what you will see under the Quick settings option:

- Tap ⏻ to quickly access Power off, Emergency mode, and Restart options

- Tap 🔍 (Finder) to search the device for an item.

- Tap ⚙ (Open settings) to access the full device settings.

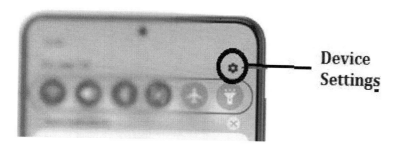

Device
Settings

- Tap ⋮ (More options) to modify Quick settings/button layout.

Tip: You can open the full settings when you touch and hold a quick setting icon.

Wireless Power Sharing

Your Samsung S21 Ultra is capable of wirelessly charging other compatible Samsung devices. It is also worthy of knowing that wireless power-sharing (charging) works with most Qi-Certified devices.

Note: Your device must be at least 30% charged to share power.

→ Go to *Settings* > tap (Battery and device care) > *Battery* > *Wireless power sharing*

In order not to exhaust your device battery, set a battery charge limit.

→ Tap *Battery limit*, then choose a percentage in which you want the charging to stop. (Once the device attains this charge level, the power-sharing turns off automatically).

→ Next, turn on the charging feature by tapping .

→ Place the phone so that it faces down, then place the oncoming device on the back.

You will get notified when the charging begins.

Tip: If you have issues connecting with a compatible device, you might have to remove any covering/accessories that might be obstructing the devices.

Warning: Do not use headphones while charging using wireless power-sharing.

Meet the Virtual Assistant: Bixby

Bixby is a Samsung developed virtual assistant. It is your virtual assistant that is made to learn your routines and what you like, evolves and helps you to execute tasks on your device.

You can interact with Bixby just like with Siri on Apple devices.

Accessing Bixby

To access Bixby, from a Home screen, press and hold the Side key. (Except you have changed Side key press and hold command to open Power off menu).

Alternatively, Bixby can also be accessed from the Apps list.

Bixby Routines

Bixby Routines gives you information based on where you are and probably what you are doing. It can also change your device settings based on your location or what you are doing.

→ Go to *Settings* > tap (*Advanced features*) > *Bixby Routines*

Bixby Vision

Bixby gives you more insight into what you see on your Camera, Gallery, and Internet apps. It is integrated into these apps. It is brilliant in QR code detection and landmark recognition.

Let's see how Bixby Vision works with Camera, Gallery and the Internet.

Camera

You can find the Bixby Vision on the Camera viewfinder which helps you to understand what you see.

When you open (Camera), tap *More*, and then *Bixby Vision*. Follow the prompts from here.

Gallery

→ Go to (Gallery), and tap a picture.

→ Tap (Bixby Vision), and follow the onscreen prompts.

Internet

Using the Internet app, you can find more information about an image through the help of Bixby Vision.

→ From (Internet), touch and hold an image, and then tap *Search with Bixby Vision* from the pop-up menu.

Harnessing the Biometric Security Feature on Your Device

The biometrics feature enables you to securely unlock your device as well as granting you access to certain accounts. To secure your device, you can use Face recognition and/or Fingerprint scanner.

Using Face Recognition

You can enable Face recognition to unlock your device screen; this means you can use your face to unlock your device.

Note: Face recognition feature is less secure compared to the use of Pattern, Password/PIN. Therefore, you will be required to setup Pattern, Password or PIN regardless of setting up Face recognition.

How to register Face recognition

→ Go to *Settings* > tap ⬤ (Biometrics and security) > *Face recognition*

→ Follow the onscreen instructions on steps to register your face.

Note: When you are registering your face for Biometric, avoid wearing glasses, heavy make-up, face mask, cap. Also, make sure that you register your face in a well-lit area.

You can customize your Face recognition settings after enrolling your face.

• To delete existing face data, Go to *Settings* > tap ⬤ (Biometrics and security) > *Face recognition* > *Remove face data.*

• You can enable or disable the face recognition security by going through this path: *Settings* > tap ⬤ (Biometrics and security) > *Face recognition* > *Face unlock.*

• If you want facial recognition to recognize your face only when your eyes are opened, follow this path to enable/disable: *Settings >*

tap ⬤ (Biometrics and security) > *Face recognition > Require open eyes.*

Other options available under the Face recognition settings include:

- Add alternative look
- Stay on Lock screen until swipe
- Brighten screen
- Faster recognition

Using Fingerprint scanner

The fingerprint recognition is one of the biometric security passes to access your device. The fingerprint recognition can be used in place of PIN or password. It can also be used to verify your identity when logging in to some apps and your Samsung account.

Note: You must set up a pattern, PIN, or password before you can use fingerprint recognition.

Fingerprint management (Add, remove and rename)

To add your fingerprint:

→ Go to *Settings* > tap (Biometrics and security) > *Fingerprints*

→ Follow the onscreen instructions on steps to register your fingerprint.

To delete/rename a fingerprint: As soon as you open the Fingerprint option, the list of registered fingerprints can be seen at the top of the list. To delete a fingerprint, tap the fingerprint and then choose to remove or rename it.

Mobile Continuity on Your Device

This feature enables you to access your device storage and other functions across compatible devices. Also, this feature allows you to sync your calls and messages across your Samsung devices. You can link your device to *Samsung DeX, Window devices, and other compatible devices.

---

*Samsung DeX is a feature included on some Samsung handheld devices which enable users to extend their device into a desktop experience through the connection of a keyboard, monitor and mouse.

Continuity: Link your device to Windows

You can link up your device with Windows PCs for mobile continuity. This allows you to access your device's storage files such as photos, videos, documents, messages, and more on the Windows desktop.

To link your device to your PC, follow the instruction below:

→ Go to *Settings* > *(Advanced features)* > *Link to Windows*

→ follow the onscreen prompts to complete the connection between your device and PC.

What you can do after linking your device to your Windows PC

- Drag and drop pictures from your device to Windows, but you will have to edit pictures in Your Photos app.

- Get a pop-up on Windows when you receive a new message and manage notifications from your PC.

- It allows for 'app mirroring' as you can live stream your phone screen on your PC.

- This features also allows you to interact with your phone device using the keyboard and mouse.

Continuity: Samsung DeX

With DeX, you can enjoy an enhanced multitasking experience by connecting your device to a PC or TV. Your device can be connected to a TV or monitor by using an HDMI cable or wirelessly. You can install DeX on your PC for quick and easy file transfer between your device and PC.

To enable DeX, follow the instruction below:

→ Go to *Settings* > *(Advanced features)* > *Samsung DeX* > Tap to turn on the feature.

$\rightarrow$ Follow the onscreen instructions on how to connect your device to your TV/PC.

Note: For PC connection, you will have to download the DeX app on your PC. Below is the download link; samsungdex.com

Multi-Task with Multi Window

With the Multi-window, you can use multiple apps at the same time. Supported apps can be displayed on a split-screen. You can switch between the apps and adjust the size of their windows.

→ Tap ▐▐▐ , and then tap *Recent apps*.

→ Tap the app icon you wish to open, and then tap *Open in split screen view*.

→ In the other window, tap an app to add it to the split screen view.

→ To adjust the window size, drag the middle of
the window border

Mastering Samsung Keyboard: Input Text on Your Device Like A Pro

You can enter text on your device using an onscreen keyboard or your voice. The Samsung keyboard has a toolbar where you can find several features of the keyboard.

Let's take out time to examine the toolbar which provides quick access to features of the keyboard.

The Toolbar

To access the toolbar, tap ●●● (Expand toolbar) from the Samsung keyboard to reveal the options described in the table below:

Features	Description
😊 (Emoji)	Insert an emoji
(AR Emoji)	Create personalized emojis that can be used as sharable stickers.
(Mojitok)	Create personalized stickers or insert suggested ones.

56

(GIFs)	Insert animated GIFs
(Stickers)	Insert illustrated stickers
(Search)	Locate certain words, phrases, in your conversation
(Voice input)	Use voice to input text instead of typing
(Handwriting)	Insert text using your handwriting (Galaxy S21 Ultra 5G only).
(Translate)	Translate words or sentences typed on the keyboard to another language.
(Samsung Pass)	Get secure access to apps and services using biometrics.
(YouTube)	Insert a video from YouTube
(Spotify)	Insert music from Spotify

57

⊟ (Clipboard)	Access copied text from the Clipboard
⬚ (Keyboard size)	Adjust the keyboard's height or width.
⌨ (Modes)	Select the keyboard layout
✛ (Text editing)	The text editing panel is useful when you want to select the text you want to cut or copy.
⚙ (Settings)	Access keyboard settings

Samsung voice input (Speech-to-text)

With the Samsung voice input, you can speak your text instead of typing. You have to speak as clearly as possible.

To use the voice input, tap 🎤 from the Samsung keyboard, and then speak your text. As you speak, the text is displayed on the screen. From the voice input screen, you can switch back to keyboard mode or open the settings for voice input. Check the figure below:

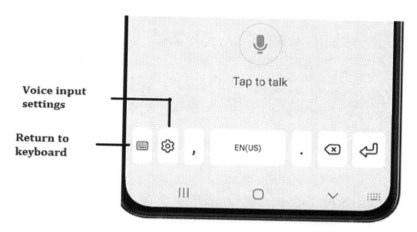

Samsung voice input settings

When using the Samsung voice input, you can customize the options by tapping ⚙ (Settings). Below are the options:

- Keyboard language
- Voice input language
- Hide offensive words

Customize the Samsung keyboard

You can configure the options for your Samsung keyboard where you can modify the keyboard language, size/transparency, font size, theme, mode, configure smart typing, predictive text, and more.

To access these options, go to the Samsung keyboard, and then tap ⚙️ (Settings) to reveal the options you might want to make changes.

Note: Galaxy S21 Ultra 5G users can customize handwriting options under this setting.

Conserve Your Battery with Emergency Mode

The Emergency mode enables you to use some vital emergency features during emergencies. Also, the emergency mode helps to conserve battery power by restricting application usage only to the applications you select, or the ones that are deemed to be essential. The Emergency mode turns off some features when the screen is off, e.g. connectivity features and Mobile data.

How to activate the Emergency mode

→ Press and hold the Volume down and the Side keys simultaneously.

→ Tap (Emergency mode)

→ Tap *Turn on*

Note: When using this feature for the first time, you are obliged to read and accept the terms and conditions before you can proceed.

Available features of the Emergency mode

The apps and features below are the only items you will find on the Home screen while in the Emergency mode. However, options may vary by carrier.

- Estimated battery life
- Flashlight
- Phone
- Internet
- Chrome Browser
- Emergency alarm
- Emergency call
- Share/Message my location

In the Emergency mode, you can tap the More option (⋮) to reveal more features such as:

- Edit: Here, you can add or remove apps from the screen.

- Emergency contacts: Manage your ICE and medical profile group contacts in case of an emergency.

- Turn off Emergency mode: when you turn off the Emergency mode, the device is restored to standard mode.

- Settings

Apps Management

Apps downloaded from the Galaxy Store and the Google Play store are displayed in the Apps list alongside preloaded apps.

How do I access the Apps list?

To access the Apps list, from a Home screen, swipe the screen upward.

Search for apps

You can search for an app or a setting relating to the app by using the Search feature.

→ Go to Apps > tap *Search*, and then enter a keyword or phrase related to the app you are looking for.

→ From the searched result, tap your desired result to go to the app.

Sort apps

You can sort app shortcuts alphabetically or in a personalized order (manually)

→ Go to Apps > tap ⋮ (More options) > *Sort*

→ From the Sorting options, you can choose:

- Custom order: Allows you to arrange apps manually.

- Alphabetical order: This sorts apps alphabetically.

Pro Tip: When using custom order, empty icon spaces can be removed. To do this, tap ⋮ (More options) > *Clean up pages*

App folders management

You can create folders for App shortcuts to make your Apps list look organized.

→ To create a folder, from Apps, touch and hold an app shortcut, then drag it unto another app shortcut until it is highlighted, and then release the app shortcut.

After creating the folder, you can add a folder name, change the folder color, and add more apps.

→ Tap *Folder name* to enter the new folder name, tap ◯ (Palette) to change folder color, tap + to add more apps in the created folder and then tap *Done* after selecting the apps.

→ Tap ‹ (Back) to close the folder.

You can copy an app folder to a Home screen, to do this, go to Apps, touch and hold a folder, and then tap ⊕ (Add to Home)

To delete an app folder, from Apps, touch and hold the folder, and then tap 🗑 (Delete folder).

Note: When you delete an app folder, the app shortcut is taken back to the Apps list.

Uninstall/disable apps

Downloaded and installed apps can be removed from your device. In contrast, *preloaded apps on your device can not be removed but can only be disabled.

*Preloaded apps are apps that come with your device by default. When disabled from your device, they are turned off and hidden from the Apps list; it doesn't mean that they are permanently removed from the device.

To uninstall or disable an app, go to Apps, touch and hold an app, and then tap *Uninstall* or *Disable*

Customize your downloaded and preloaded apps

To customize your apps option, go to Settings, and then tap (Apps).

The Camera App: The Act of Taking Picture and Videos

Using the Camera app, you can capture high-quality pictures and videos. You can access Camera from Apps.

Using the Camera app to take photos

You can navigate the camera screen to take quality pictures with your device cameras (the front and the rear).

To take a photo, open the Camera app , and then use the features below to set up your shot:

- To switch between the front and the rear cameras, you can quickly do so by swiping the screen up or down.
- If you wish to adjust the brightness, tap the screen on where you want to brighten up. The tap reveals the brightness scale and then drag the slider.
- Swipe the screen up or down to switch between shooting mode.
- Tap (Settings) to change camera settings.

When all is set, tap (Capture) to take a shot.

Customize the shooting mode

The Camera can automatically help you determine the ideal mode for your photos, or you can choose from the shooting mode.

If you are choosing your shooting mode, then read the steps and descriptions below:

To change the shooting modes, swipe the Camera screen right and left. Check below for the shooting modes:

- *Single take*: This allows you to capture multiple pictures and videos from different angles.
- *Photo*: Using this mode, the Camera determines the ideal settings for your pictures.
- *Video*: Using this mode, the Camera determines the ideal settings for your videos.
- *More*: Access other available shooting modes.

Tip: Tap ⊕ to drag modes into the shooting modes tray.

- *AR Doodle*: This is a video enhancing feature with which you can add line drawings.
- *Pro*: Customize some advanced features such as ISO sensitivity, color tone, white balance, and exposure value while taking photos.
- *Pro video*: Adjust advance settings such as ISO sensitivity, color tone, white balance, and exposure value while recording a video.
- *Panorama*: Take pictures in Panorama mode (linear vertical or horizontal images).
- *Night*: Suitable for low-light conditions without the use of a flashlight.
- *Food*: Ideal for taking food images.
- *Portrait*: Set your background for a portrait shot.

- *Portrait video*: Set your background for a portrait video.
- *Slow motion*: Videos are recorded at a high frame rate and can be viewed in slow motion.
- *Super slo*-mo: Videos are recorded at an extremely high frame rate.
- *Hyperlapse*: Make time-lapse video.
- *Director*'s view: This grants you access to more advanced features.

Scene optimizer

The Scene optimizer helps you to capture beautiful photos by adjusting some settings based on what is detected in the camera frame.

Note: Scene optimizer is not available when using the front Camera.

→ Open *Camera* 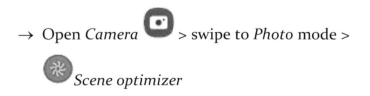 > swipe to *Photo* mode > *Scene optimizer*

<u>Note</u>: The Scene optimizer icon changes based on what the Camera detects.

Single take

This shooting mode allows you to capture more in each shot, as you can take both photos and videos simultaneously. This mode utilizes AI to create high-quality images and videos from multiple angles.

→ Open *Camera* > swipe to *Single take* mode

→ Tap and then select a timer option.

→ Tap to record and then pan around the scene to take multiple views and angles.

Space Zoom

The Space Zoom feature allows you to capture photos using high magnification (up to 100 times), giving your output much clarity and accuracy.

→ Open *Camera*

→ Tap a *Zoom shortcut* to choose a
   magnification setting.

→ Center your target in the shot frame, and
   then tap (Zoom lock) for accurate
   zoom focusing.

→ Tap ⬭ to capture.

Recording videos

→ Open *Camera* ⬤ > swipe to *Video* shooting
   mode

→ Tap ⬤ to start your video recording.
   - While recording your video, you can take
     a picture by tapping ⬤ (Capture)
   - You can pause the recording by tapping
     ⏸ , and to continue recording, tap ⬤.

→ Tap ⬛ to stop the recording.

Video Zoom-in mic

When recording a video in the Video mode, and you zoom in on an audio source, it is important that you increase the volume of the sound and minimize the background noise.

Note: This feature cannot be used with the front Camera or other video modes

→ Open *Camera* > tap (Settings) > *Advanced recording options > Zoom-in mic*

→ Tap to enable

→ To return to the main Camera screen, tap .

→ On the Camera main screen, swipe to change the mode to *Video.*

→ Tap to commence recording; while recording, zoom in or out on the audio source.

75

Note: The microphone icon indicates the level of amplification being applied.

The camera settings

You can configure your camera settings by using the icons on the main Camera as well as the settings menu:

→ From the Camera app 📷 , tap ⚙ (Settings) to access the following options:

- *Swipe Shutter button to*: When you swipe the shutter to the nearest edge, choose whether you want the action to be taking a burst shot or creating a GIF.

- *Format and advanced options*: Select the format in which you want your file to be saved and other saving options.

- *Scene optimizer*: Tap this to allow automatic adjustment to the color settings of your pictures relatively to the subject matter.

- *Shot suggestions*: This presents onscreen guides giving you tips on how to make great shots.

- *Scan QR codes*: Detect QR codes automatically when using the Camera.
- *Use wide angle for group selfies*: Automatically switch to wide-angle when a selfie is involving two or people.
- *Save selfies as previewed*
- Selfie color tone
- *Auto HDR*: Capture extra details in your shots, especially in the bright and dark areas.
- *Tracking auto-focus*: Detects a moving subject and keeps it in focus.
- *Grid lines*: Shows viewfinder grid lines
- *Location tags*: Adds a GPS location tag to your photos and videos.
- *Shooting methods*: User can choose to take pictures or record video using the available options.
- *Settings to keep*: Choose whether to keep the previous settings you used the last time you launch Camera or not.
- *Shutter sound*: Play a sound when taking a photo.

- *Vibration feedback*: Enable vibrations when tapping the screen while using the Camera app.
- Reset settings: Reset Camera settings to its default.

Gallery

The Gallery is the site to view, edit and manage your pictures and videos. The Gallery allows you to view all visual media stored on your device.

→ To access Gallery; from Apps, tap (Gallery)

View pictures from Gallery

All pictures stored on your device can be viewed in Gallery.

→ From (Gallery) > *Pictures*

→ To view a picture, tap it. Once a picture is opened, swipe right or left to view other pictures or videos.

From the picture screen, you can:

- Use Bixby Vision on the picture in view; tap *Bixby Vision*

- Mark the picture in view as a favorite by tapping ♡ (Add to Favorites)

Tap ⋮ (More options) to access other features such as:

- *Details*: See and modify information about the picture in view.
- *Set as wallpaper*: Set the picture in view as wallpaper.
- *Copy to Clipboard*: Copy the picture so you can paste into another app.
- *Move to Secure Folder*
- *Print*

Play video from Gallery

→ From (Gallery) > Pictures
→ When you locate a video, tap the video to view it, and swipe either right or left to view other videos or pictures.

- When you view a video, you can mark it as a favorite by tapping ♡ (Add to Favorites). Videos marked as Favorites are added to Favorites in the Albums tab.

- You can access more features by tapping ⋮ (More options):
  - *Details*: See and modify information about the video.
  - *Set as wallpaper*: Use the video as the Lock screen wallpaper.
  - *Move to Secure Folder*

→ Tap ▶ to play the selected video.

Pro Tip: You can enhance the image quality of your videos, giving you more color clarity. From *Settings* > tap 🔆 (Advanced features) > *Video enhancer* > tap ⬤ to enable.

Use Gallery to edit pictures

The Gallery app has some editing tools that help enhance your pictures.

→ From (Gallery) > *Pictures*

→ Tap a picture to view it, while on the picture screen, tap (Edit) to reveal the following options:

- *Transform*: Make changes to the overall appearance of the picture such as rotating, flipping, cropping and some other alterations.

- *Filters*: Add color effects

- *Tone*: Make adjustment to the exposure, contrast, brightness and more.

- *Draw*: Insert hand-drawn or handwritten content.

- *Text*: Add text

- Stickers: Overlay stickers

- *Portrait*: Enhance facial features.

- *Auto adjust*: Apply automatic adjustment to enhance the picture.

- *Revert*: Discard all changes applied.

→ Tap *Save* when done.

Video Editing

Videos that are stored on your device can be edited from the Galley app.

→ From (Gallery) > *Pictures*

→ When you locate a video, tap the video to view it

→ To access the editing tools, tap (Edit):

- *Trim*: Cut out some segments from the video.

- *Transform*: Make changes to the video's appearance such as rotation, cropping, flipping and more.

- *Filters*: Insert visual effects into the video.

- *Sticker*: Overlay stickers (illustrated or animated).

- *Draw*: Making a drawing on your video

- *Text*: Customize and insert text to your video

- *Speed*: Customize the play speed of your video.

- *Audio*: Insert background music into your video, and adjust the volume level.

- *Play*: Preview the video that has been edited.

→ After you edit and preview, to save your final output, tap *Save*.

How to delete pictures and videos

→ From (Gallery) > tap (More options) > *Edit*

→ Tap the pictures or videos you wish to delete.

→ Tap to delete the selected items.

How to share pictures and videos from Gallery

→ From (Gallery) > *Pictures*

→ Tap (More options) > *Edit*; select the item you want to share.

→ Tap (Share)

→ Choose from the list of apps or connection to share your selected item(s).

Capture a screenshot

Create an image of any portion of your screen.

→ Press and release the Side and Volume down keys.

An album is automatically created for Screenshots in the Gallery app.

Pro Tip: You can take a screenshot by swiping the edge of your hand across the screen from side to side.

→ Settings > tap (Advanced features) > *Motions and gestures > Palm swipe to capture.*

→ Tap to enable this feature.

Screenshot settings

You can modify your screenshot settings from *Settings* > tap (Advanced features) > *Screenshots and screen recorder*

Below are some of the customized settings you can find:

- *Hide status and navigation bars*: When you select this option, your device's navigation bars or status bar will not be displayed on your screenshot.
- *Screenshot format*: Choose if you want your screenshot to be saved in JPG or PNG files.
- *Screenshot toolbar*: Display more options after taking a screenshot.
- *Delete shared screenshots*: Screenshots are deleted automatically after they are shared through the screenshot toolbar.

Screen recording

With screen recording, you can record activities on your device and record a video overlay of yourself using the Camera.

→ From <u>Quick settings</u> > tap 　　 (Screen recorder)> *Start recording*

→ As soon as you tap Start recording, a countdown runs for three seconds before the recording begins. However, you skip the countdown by tapping *Skip countdown*.

→ Tap to stop recording.

- While executing a screen recording on your device, you can draw on the screen by tapping .

- You can record yourself using the front Camera while recording your screen by tapping .

Note: Screen recordings are automatically saved in the Screen recordings album in the Gallery app.

Screen recording settings

→ Settings > tap (Advanced features) > tap *Screenshots and screen recorder*; *tap* to customize any of the following options:

- *Sound*: Choose the kind of sounds to be captured in the screen recording.
- *Selfie video size*: Set the size of the video overlay by dragging the slider.
- Video quality: Choose a resolution for the screen recording file size.

Exploring Samsung Apps

The Samsung apps center presents you with some apps that are exclusive to your device alone. You can also access and download a collection of premium content.

Galaxy Essentials

The Galaxy Essentials captures a collection of specially selected applications available on Samsung apps.

To access Galaxy Essentials, from Apps, tap ⋮ (More options), and then *Galaxy Essentials*.

AR Zone

Access all AR features from this app. It keeps all the features in one place for easy accessibility.

Bixby

Bixby is a Samsung developed virtual assistant. It is your virtual assistant that is made to learn your routines and what you like, evolves and helps you to execute tasks on your device. Bixby shows customized content based on your interactions with the device. (For more information on Bixby, refer to Accessing Bixby).

Galaxy Shop

With the Galaxy Shop app, you can stay updated with the upcoming Galaxy device, shop for Samsung products, as well as unlocking exclusive offers.

Galaxy Store

To download from the Galaxy Store, you need a Samsung account (Refer to Add a Samsung Account to your device). You can access and download premium apps that are specifically designed for Galaxy devices.

Galaxy Wearable

This app is needed to connect your Samsung Watch to your device.

Game Launcher

The Game Launcher app helps you to arrange all your games in one place. If you can't find Game Launcher in your Apps list, you can add it from

Settings > (Advanced features) > *Game Launcher*; then tap ⬤.

PENUP

This is handy for those using the S Pen to sketch, draw, scribble or paint.

Samsung Free

This gives you access to exclusive TV live shows, news, and articles from different sources and free interactive games.

Samsung Global Goals

Get more information about the Global Goals initiative and contribute by donating towards this cause.

Samsung Members

To use this app, you must be a Samsung member. It allows you to do more with your Galaxy device and access exclusive content and experiences.

Samsung TV Plus

This offers news and entertainment contents all for free.

SmartThings

This apps allows you to control and manage connected devices. You can see the status of the connected devices through the dashboard.

Settings Center

The Settings allows you to customize your device to your taste.

Quick Tips:

+ Accessing Settings from a Home screen: Swipe down and tap ⚙ (Settings)

+ Accessing Setting from Apps: tap ◉ (Settings)

+ You can search for a specific setting if you are not sure where it is. From Settings, proceed to tap 🔍 (Search), and enter the search term. From the results, tap an entry to go to the setting.

Manage Your Connections Settings

We will be examining settings related to wireless connections such as Wi-Fi, Bluetooth, Mobile networks, Mobile Hotspot, Tethering, and Network settings.

Bluetooth

The Bluetooth feature enables you to pair your device with other Bluetooth-supported devices. Connecting with a Bluetooth device for the first time, you must pair the device with your device.

Pairing your device with another Bluetooth-enabled device

To pair your device with another Bluetooth device, ensure that Bluetooth is turned on for both devices and it must be in discoverable mode.

→ Settings > tap (Connections) > *Bluetooth* > tap to turn Bluetooth on

→ Tap the device you wish to connect with and follow the prompts to pair and connect with the device.

Tip: To share a file using Bluetooth, you have to tap Bluetooth.

Rename a paired Bluetooth device

A paired device appears on your list of paired devices, and usually, it bears the name of the device. You can decide to rename it for easy recognition.

→ Settings > tap (Connections) > *Bluetooth* > tap to turn Bluetooth on

→ Proceed to tap (Settings) which can be found next to the device name, and then tap *Rename.*

→ Modify the name, and tap *Rename*.

Unpair a Bluetooth device from your phone

Unpairing from a Bluetooth device means your phone won't connect automatically with the device when they are within a Bluetooth range, and both are turned on.

To unpair;

→ Settings > tap (Connections) > *Bluetooth* > tap to turn Bluetooth on

→ Proceed to tap (Settings) which can be found next to the device name, and then tap *Unpair*.

Accessing Advanced Bluetooth options

You can get access to additional Bluetooth features from the Advanced menu. From these options, you can change your device name for Bluetooth connections, view a list of received files from Bluetooth connections, sync with

Samsung cloud, view apps that have recently used Bluetooth, and many more.

To access these additional Bluetooth features, go to;

→ Settings > tap 📶 (Connections) > *Bluetooth*

→ Tap ⋮ (More options) > *Advanced*

Play audio on your device to two connected Bluetooth audio devices

→ Connect the Bluetooth audio devices to your phone, respectively.

→ From your phone Notification panel, tap *Media*, then under *Audio output*, tap ✅ next to the audio devices. (Max of two devices allowed).

Wi-Fi

You can connect your device to the internet without using mobile data, one of the ways you can do that is using a Wi-Fi network.

Connect your device to a Wi-Fi network

→ *Settings >* (Connections) > *Wi-Fi* > tap

to turn Wi-Fi on

→ when you turn Wi-Fi on, it automatically scans for available networks, tap a network, and then enter the password to access the network (if required).

Connect your device to a hidden Wi-Fi network

Sometimes, a Wi-Fi network administrator may decide to hide their Wi-Fi network from being listed after turning on your Wi-Fi and completing a scan. However, you can connect to the network by inputting the network information manually.

→ *Settings >* (Connections) > *Wi-Fi* > tap

to turn Wi-Fi on

→ At the bottom of the list, tap *Add network*.

→ Input the Wi-Fi network information:

- *Network name*: Input the name of the network (It must be exact)
- *Security*: Choose the security type, and then enter the password (if required)
- *Advanced*: Address IP and Proxy settings.

→ Tap *Save* to complete the process.

Note: You need to request the Wi-Fi network name and password from the administrator, and other information.

Pro Tip: If a Wi-Fi network is secured with a QR code, you can scan the QR code using your device by tapping ▣ QR scanner button to connect to the Wi-Fi network.

Advanced Wi-Fi network settings

The Wi-Fi network advanced settings allow you to configure and manage connections to different Wi-Fi networks and hotspots. To access the advanced Wi-Fi network and what you can do from there, check below:

→ *Settings* > (Connections) > *Wi-Fi* > tap

to turn Wi-Fi on

→ Tap (More options) > *Advanced*

From the Advanced options, you can do any of the following:

- *Network notification/Wi-Fi notifications*: Get notified when an open network in range is detected.

- *Switch to mobile data*: Enabling this feature will ensure that your device will switch to mobile data whenever the Wi-Fi connection is weak or unstable. It automatically switches back to the Wi-Fi connection when it becomes stable/strong.

- *Show network quality info:* Access network information

- *Detect suspicious networks:* This notifies you of suspicious and malicious activity on your current Wi-Fi network when detected.

- *Wi-Fi control history:* Check for apps that have recently turned on/off your Wi-Fi

- *Hotspot 2.0:* Connect to Wi-Fi networks that support Hotspot 2.0 automatically.
- *Turn on Wi-Fi automatically*
- *Manage network*
- *Wi-Fi power saving mode*
- *Show Wi-Fi pop-up*

Wi-Fi Direct

You can share data between devices by using Wi-Fi Direct.

→ *Settings >* 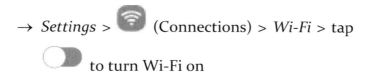 (Connections) > *Wi-Fi* > tap to turn Wi-Fi on

→ Tap ⋮ (More options) > *Wi-Fi Direct*

→ To connect to a device, tap the device and follow the prompts

To disconnect from Wi-Fi Direct,

→ *Settings >* (Connections) > *Wi-Fi* > tap to turn Wi-Fi on

→ Tap ⁝ (More options) > *Wi-Fi Direct;* tap a device to disconnect it.

Mobile hotspot

You can use your device as a mobile hotspot for other devices, which means you can share your device data plan with multiple devices by creating a Wi-Fi network from which they can connect.

To set up your Mobile hotspot connection, follow the steps below:

→ *Settings* > 📶 (Connections) >*Mobile hotspot and tethering > Mobile hotspot*

→ Tap ⬤ to turn on your device Mobile hotspot.

→ Turn on the Wi-Fi of the device you wish to connect to your device Mobile hotspot, select your device's Mobile hotspot from the list of available Wi-Fi networks; and then connect by entering the Mobile hotspot password.

Note: You can change the default network name and password for your device's Mobile hotspot.

Tip: You can view connected devices under the heading *Connected devices.*

Edit your Mobile hotspot password

Your device Mobile hotspot uses a default password until you change it. It's good to change the password to the one you can remember easily.

→ *Settings >* *(Connections) >Mobile hotspot and tethering > Mobile hotspot*

→ Tap the password field, input a new password, and tap *Save.*

Mobile hotspot settings configuration

→ *Settings >* *(Connections) > Mobile hotspot and tethering > Mobile hotspot*

→ Tap *Configure* to reveal the following settings:

- *Network name*: View and change your device Mobile hotspot name.
- *Security*: Select the security type for your Mobile Hotspot.
- *Password*: View and change your password.
- *Band*: Select a bandwidth option.
- *Advanced*: Access additional Mobile hotspot settings.

From your device, you can automatically share your hotspot connection with devices signed into your Samsung account.

→ *Settings >* (Connections) > *Mobile hotspot and tethering > Mobile hotspot*

→ Tap *Auto hotspot*, and tap to enable.

Tethering

Tethering can be used to share your device's internet connection with another device using wireless or wired connections using either

Bluetooth tethering, USB tethering or Ethernet tethering.

Note: Options may vary by carrier

To access the *Tethering* option, go to *Settings* > (Connections) > *Mobile hotspot and tethering.* From here, you can tap an option from the list below:

- *Bluetooth tethering*: This enables you to share your device's internet connection using Bluetooth.
- *USB tethering*: This enables you to share your device's internet with your computer using a USB cable.
- Ethernet tethering: This enables you to share your device's internet with your computer using Ethernet adapter.

Mobile networks

Configure your device to connect to mobile networks and use mobile data. To access Mobile networks, go to *Settings* > tap ⬜ (Connections) > *Mobile networks*

Under the *Mobile networks* option, you can get the following settings:

- *Mobile data*: Enable mobile data usage to access the internet.
- *International data roaming*: Change settings for international roaming
- *Allow 2G service*: Allow the use of 2G service during limited cellular coverage.
- *Data roaming*: while you are outside your carrier's network area, choose whether to allow your device to connect to mobile data.
- *Data roaming access*: Setup access to mobile network during roaming.
- *Roaming/Roaming state*: Enable/Disable data while roaming on another mobile network.
- *Signal strength*: Check the mobile signal strength
- *Enhanced Calling*: Using LTE data, enable enhanced communication

- *Network mode*: Select network modes.

- *Access points*: Select or add APNs.

- *Network operators*: Select available and preferred networks.

Manage Data usage

You can track and manage your mobile and Wi-Fi data usage, as well as customizing the data limits and warnings.

→ *Settings* > tap 📶 (Connections) > *Data usage*

From the *Data usage* option, you can turn on/off Data saver, monitor mobile and Wi-Fi data, as well as roaming data usage.

Data saver

When Data saver is enabled, it reduces your data consumption by restricting selected apps from sending or receiving background data.

→ *Settings* > tap 📶 (Connections) > *Data usage* > *Data saver*

→ Tap to turn on this feature.

Tip: You can allow some apps to have unrestricted access to data usage while Data saver is enabled. From the *Data saver* option, tap *'Allowed to use data while in Data saver'* and then tap next to the app you want to grant this access to.

Mobile data management

You can customize and monitor your mobile data by setting data limits and restrictions to avoid excessive and unwanted data consumption.

→ *From Settings >* *(Connections) > Data usage,* you will be able to access the following options:

- *Mobile data*: Mobile data will be used from your plan
- *International data roaming*: Mobile data services will be active while roaming internationally.

- *Mobile data only apps*: Select the apps that will use mobile data.
- *Mobile data usage*: View data usage used with mobile connections.
- *Alert me about data usage*: Enable to get notified when your mobile data usage reached the specific volume.
- *Billing cycle and data warning*: Alter the monthly date to correspond with your carrier's billing date.

Wi-Fi/ Roaming data usage

You can also monitor the Wi-Fi data usage as well as restricting the Wi-Fi data access.

→ *Settings* > tap (Connections) > *Data usage*

→ To view data usage over Wi-Fi connections, tap *Wi-Fi data usage*

For roaming data usage;

→ *Settings* > tap 📶 (Connections) > *Data usage* > *Roaming data usage*

Airplane mode

When Airplane mode is turned on, all network connections are turned off. While in the Airplane mode, you can turn on Bluetooth and Wi-Fi in Settings. You can't make or receive calls, text messages or use mobile data while in Airplane mode.

→ *Settings* > tap 📶 (Connections) > *Airplane mode*

→ To enable this feature, tap ⬭.

Tip: You can turn on Airplane mode from Quick settings

NFC (Near Field Communication)/payment

Without connecting to a network, your phone can communicate with another device through Near Field Communication (NFC).

Note: The other device must support NFC and needs to be within a range of four centimeters with your device.

NFC is used by some payment apps.

→ *Settings* > tap 📶 (Connections) > *NFC and contactless payments* > tap ⬭ to turn on

Using NFC to make payments

Note: The NFC technology is used with Samsung Pay.

Samsung Pay is a mobile payment and digital wallet service that allows users to make payments using Samsung devices and other compatible phones. With Samsung Pay, you can add your credit and debit cards to your device.

You can use an NFC payment app to make payments by touching your device to a compatible credit card reader.

→ *Settings* > tap (Connections) > *NFC and contactless payments* > tap to turn on.

→ To see the default payment app, tap *Contactless payments.*

- If you wish to change the payment app, tap an available app to select it.
- Tap *Pay with currently open app* to use an open payment app.
- To choose another payment service, tap *Others,* then tap the service you want to use as the default payment service.

Nearby device scanning

Nearby device scanning is a feature that sends you a notification when there are devices available to connect to, hence making it easier to set up connections to available devices.

→ *Settings* > tap 📶 (Connections) > *More connection settings* > *Nearby device scanning.*

→ To turn on this feature, tap ⬤▬

Virtual Private Network (VPN)

From your device, you can connect to a private secured network via VPN. You will need the connection details from the VPN administrator to connect to the network securely.

→ *Settings* > tap 📶 (Connections) > *More connection settings* > *VPN*

→ Tap ⋮ (More options) > *Add VPN profile*

→ Enter the VPN information as provided by the administrator

→ Tap *Save.*

Connect your device wirelessly to a printer

To connect your device to a printer, they have to be on the same Wi-Fi network. When connected, you can print documents and images on your device on the printer.

→ *Settings* > tap ⬤ (Connections) > *More connection settings* > *Printing*

→ Tap *Default print service*

→ Tap ⋮ (More options) > *Add printer*

If your printer needs a plugin to add a print service, tap ➕ (Download plugin) and follow the instructions.

Display Settings

You can customize your device settings to suit your preferences. The display settings allow you to adjust your screen brightness, set theme, font size, timeout delay, touch sensitivity, and many other settings associated with the display.

Adjust Screen brightness

The screen brightness can be adjusted to adapt automatically to the lighting condition of your environment. You can also adjust it manually to suit your preference.

To adjust your device screen brightness, go to:

→ *Settings* > tap (Display) > *Brightness*

Under *Brightness* settings, you can access the Brightness slider as well as the Adaptive brightness option.

- To set the brightness level manually, drag the Brightness slider either to the right (increase) or to the left (decrease)

- If you want screen brightness to adjust automatically based on your environment's lighting conditions, tap *Adaptive brightness.*

Pro Tip: You can manually adjust the screen brightness from the Quick settings panel.

Adjust Screen resolution

You can adjust the screen resolution of your Galaxy S21 Ultra 5G device. Increasing the resolution will sharpen your device image quality while lowering it will save battery power.

→ *Settings* > tap (Display) > *Screen resolution*

→ Tap a resolution you prefer, and then tap *Apply.*

Note: Some apps may close when you change the screen resolution as they do not support higher or lower screen resolution settings.

Display Font size and style

Customize your device by changing the font style and the font size (size of text).

To change your font style, go to:

→ *Settings* > tap (Display) > *Font size and style* > *Font style*

→ Tap a font from the enlisted to select it. To add fonts from Galaxy Store, tap ✚ *(Download font)*.

Note: If you want all fonts to appear with bold weight, tap *Bold font*

→ To adjust the size of text (font size), drag the Font size slider

Dark mode

With the Dark mode, you can switch to a darker theme which is highly recommendable at night. The Dark mode darkens bright screens and notifications to keep your eyes more comfortable with the screen.

From Settings > tap ☀ (Display) to access the following options:

- *Light*: This is the default option; it applies a color theme to your device.
- *Dark*: This applies a dark color theme to your device.
- *Dark mode settings*: Set when you want Dark mode to be applied on your device. You can choose a custom schedule, or allow your device to apply it automatically using sunset and sunrise zonal timing.

Protect your eyes with Eye comfort shield

To protect your eyes against the light from your device, especially at night, the eye comfort shield helps reduce eye strain.

→ *Settings* > tap ☀ (Display) > *Eye comfort shield*

→ To enable the feature, tap ⬤, and then tap any of the options below:
  - *Adaptive*: This automatically adjusts your screen color temperature depending on the time of the day or usage pattern.
  - *Custom*: Set the time of the day when you want Eye comfort shield to be activated. Tap *Set schedule* and select an option.

Screen light timeout

Customize the time after which your device screen turns off.

→ *Settings* > tap ☀ (Display) > *Screen timeout*

→ Tap the time limit you wish to set.

Set Screen Zoom

Increasing the zoom level is beneficial to the individual with short sight. To adjust the zoom level, follow the steps below:

→ *Settings* > tap (Display) > *Screen zoom*

→ To adjust the zoom level, drag the Screen zoom slider to the right (increase) or the left (decrease).

Screen saver

Screen saver allows you to display photos or colors when your device screen turns off or during charging.

→ *Settings* > tap (Display) > *Screen saver*

→ Under the *Screen saver* settings, choose one of the options:

  - Tap *None* if you don't want a screen saver display

- Tap *Colors* and then tap the selector to show a changing screen of colors.
- Tap *Photo table* to reveal pictures in a photo table.
- Tap *Photo frame* to display pictures in a photo frame.
- Tap Photos to display pictures from your Google Photos.

→ Tap *Preview* to check out the screen saver

Display Settings under Advanced features

- To turn on the screen by lifting your device, go to *Settings* > tap (Advanced features) > *Motions and gestures* > *Lift to wake*; enable the feature from here.
- If you want your screen to turn on by double-tapping the screen instead of using the Side key, go to *Settings* > tap (Advanced features) > *Motions and gestures* > *Double tap*

to turn on screen; you can also enable *Double tap to turn off screen* using the same path.

Other display settings

Accidental touch protection

This prevents your screen from responding to touch input while the device is in a place such as your bag or pocket where it is susceptible to accidental touch.

To enable this feature, go to *Settings* > tap (Display) > *Accidental touch protection*

Touch sensitivity

To increase the touch sensitivity of your touch input on the screen while using screen protectors, go to *Settings* > tap (Display) > *Touch sensitivity*

Display charging information

If you want your battery level and estimated charge time to be displayed when your screen is off, go to *Settings* > tap (Display) > *Show charging information.*

Sounds/Notifications Settings

Sounds and vibration

Sound mode

Under the *Sounds and vibration* settings option, you can change the sound mode without using the volume keys.

→ *Settings* > tap (Sounds and vibration)

→ Select an option from the modes: *Sound, Vibrate* or *Mute*

- You can select *Vibrate while ringing* to set your device to vibrate while ringing during an incoming call.

- With the *Vibrate* mode, your device only vibrates for notifications and alerts.

- When you choose Mute, your device gives no sound for notifications and alerts.

- If you want to set the mute period, i.e. set a limit for muting the device, tap *Temporary mute.*

Pro Tip: You can mute your device by turning the device over or covering the screen with your palm.

→ *Settings >* (Advanced features) > *Motions and gestures > Mute with gestures >* tap to enable

Volume

To set the volume level for your call notifications, media sound, and system sounds, go to *Settings* > tap (Sounds and vibration) > *Volume*; and drag the slider to adjust each sound.

Selecting a Ringtone for your device

You can use any of the preset sounds or an audio file as your device call ringtone.

→ *Settings* > tap (Sounds and vibration) > *Ringtone*

→ Tap a ringtone to preview and choose it (If you want to use an audio file, tap).

Notification sound

To set sounds for notification alerts,

→ *Settings* > tap (Sounds and vibration) > *Notification sound*

→ Tap a sound to hear how it sound, and then tap again to select it.

Tip: If you want to set a unique notification sound for each app, you can do so from the App settings menu.

System sound

From the *System sound* setting, you can choose a sound for actions such as charging, touch interactions, and more. To access *System sound*, go to;

→ *Settings* > tap (Sounds and vibration) > *System sound*

→ From the *System sound* setting, choose an available option.

Sound quality and effects

You can customize your device sound quality and effects for clearer, enhanced and high-resolution sound output.

→ *Settings* > tap (Sounds and vibration) > *Sound quality and effects*

→ Tap one of the options below:

- *Dolby Atmos*: Tap to enjoy Dolby Atmos quality sound.

- *Equalizer*: Tap to choose an audio preset or customize your audio settings.

- *UHQ upscaler*: Enhance the sound resolution of your sounds from music and videos. Tap this option to choose an upscaling option.

- *Adapt sound*: Tap this option to set a sound for your right and left ear to enhance your listening.

Notifications settings

You can customize and prioritize how apps send notifications and how you get your notification alert.

Notification pop-up style

This setting enables you to alter the style and extra settings for your notifications.

→ *Settings* > tap (Notifications); then select a pop-up style as described below:

- *Detailed:* Activate Samsung Notification settings

- *Brief*: Customize your notification colors and lighting style

- *Brief pop-*up settings: Enable customization of colors, Edge lighting style, as well as enabling notifications to display while the screen is off.

- *Included apps*: Access brief notifications for your apps.

Do not disturb

You can block sounds and notification when you enable the *Do not disturb* mode. However, you can set exceptions for contacts, apps, and alarms.

→ *Settings* > tap (Notifications) > *Do not disturb*

→ From the available options, tap to customize:

- *Do not disturb*: Block all sounds and notifications.

- *Add schedule*: Make a new schedule when you want to put your device in *Do not disturb* mode.

- *For how long*?: When you enable Do not disturb mode manually, this option allows you to choose a default duration.

- *Sleeping*: Set a schedule for Do not disturb mode during your sleep hours.

- *Apps*: Select apps that you wish to receive notifications from while in Do Not Disturb mode.

- *Alarms and sounds*: While Do not disturb is active, sounds and vibrations are enabled for events, alarms and reminders.
- *Calls, messages, and conversations*: Tap to allow exceptions for Do not disturb.
- *Hide notifications*: View more customization options on how to hide notifications.

Alert when phone picked up

When you enable this, you will be notified with a vibration when you have missed calls or messages whenever you pick up your phone.

To enable, go to Settings > (Advanced features) > *Motions and gestures* > *Alert when phone picked up*

Notifications Advanced settings

To access the advanced settings for

notifications, go to *Settings* >

(Notifications) > *Advanced settings*

Security and Lock Screen Settings

Setting a screen lock can help you secure your device.

Let's examine the screen lock types

Screen lock

The security level for each screen lock types ranges from high to medium and to no security. You can choose the most secure security level-Password, PIN, to medium such as Pattern, and no security such as Swipe and None.

How to set a secure screen lock

The most recommendable and secure screen lock types are the Pattern, PIN or Password. To set biometric locks, you are expected to set up either PIN, Pattern, or Password.

→ *Settings,* *(Lock screen) > Screen lock type*

→ Tap any of the screen lock types you wish to use

→ Tap ⬭ to enable notification display while on the lock screen. Then proceed to the following available options:

- *Icons only*: Display only notification icon in the lock screen without any extra details.

- *Details*: Notification details are displayed on the lock screen.

- *Hide content*: Notifications are not shown in the Notification panel.

- *Notifications to show*: This allows you to select the notifications shown on the lock screen.

- *Show on Always On Display*: Allows notifications display on the *Always on Display* screen.

→ To configure the screen lock options, tap to customize the following:

- *Smart Lock*: Smart Lock automatically unlock your device when certain conditions are detected. Some of these conditions are trusted locations or detection of other devices.

- *Secure lock settings*: Modify your secure lock settings if you enable a secure screen lock.

- *Always On Display*: Enable *Always On Display*. (Refer to Always On Display (AOD))

Configure your Lock screen display

The Lock screen can accommodate features such as clock, widget, contact information, shortcuts and more.

→ *From Settings* > tap 🔒 (Lock screen) to access the following options:

- *Wallpaper services*: This allows you to add additional features to your Lock screen.

- *Clock style*: Select the clock type and color

- *Widgets*: Get access to useful information by enabling widgets on the Lock screen.

- *Contact information*: Display your contact information on the Lock screen.

- Notifications: Choose the kind of notifications to be displayed on your Lock screen and AOD screen.

- *Shortcuts*: Choose the apps shortcuts you want to add to the Lock screen.

.

Accessibility Settings

The accessibility settings are designed for those who require help hearing or seeing. It provides support hence making the device easier to operate for anyone.

TalkBack

TalkBack allows you to use some controls and settings to navigate the screen without seeing the screen.

→ *Settings >* *(Accessibility) > TalkBack*

→ Tap to enable, and then tap an option from the list to customize:

- *Talkback shortcut*: Choose a shortcut with which you can turn on TalkBack quickly.
- *Settings*: Customize TalkBack settings to suit your preferences.

Enhancing visibility

Colors and clarity

The screen elements, text colors and contrast of your device can be adjusted to easier viewing.

→ Go to *Settings* > (Accessibility) > *Visibility enhancements*; and then tap an option:

- *High contrast theme*: Modify the colors and fonts to increase the contrast.
- *High contrast fonts*: Make an adjustment to the color and fonts outline to increase the contrast and background.
- *High contrast keyboard*: Make adjustment to the Samsung keyboard size and change the colors to create an increased contrast between the keyboard keys and background.
- *Highlight buttons*: Buttons are shown with a shaded background, as this will make them have a striking effect against the wallpaper.

- *Color inversion*: Change the display of colors.
- *Color adjustment*: Adjust the color of the screen if you are having difficulties seeing some colors.
- *Add color filter*: Adjust to the screen colors if it is difficult reading the text.
- *Remove animations*: Remove certain animations from the screen.
- *Magnifier window*: Magnify the screen contents.
- *Font size and style*: To configure screen fonts.
- *Screen zoom*: To configure the zoom level of your screen.
- *Screen zoom*:
- *Magnification*: Navigate through the screen using gestures such as double pinching, triple-tapping, dragging two fingers across the screen.

Hearing enhancements

→ *Settings* > (Accessibility) > *Hearing enhancements*; tap any of the following options:

- *Real time text*: To activate RTT calls.
- *Hearing aid support*: Improve the sound quality of the hearing aids.
- *Amplify ambient sound*: Amplify the sounds of your conversations by connecting headphones to your device.
- *Adapt sound*: Enhance your listening experience by customizing the sound for each ear.
- *Left/left sound balance*: Adjust the left and right balance in stereo mode.
- *Mono audio*: Use mono for one earphone.
- *Mute all sounds*: Enable to turn off all audio and notifications.

You can find other options for text display such as;

- *Live Transcribe*: Record speech using a microphone and convert the speech to text.
- *Live Caption*: Caption speech automatically in media played on your device.
- *Google subtitles (CC)*: To configure subtitle services and closed caption.

S Pen

The Galaxy S21 Ultra 5G supports the S Pen. It provides a range of helpful functions such as launching of apps, notes taking, drawing of pictures, and more.

Note: The S Pen is sold separately and doesn't come with your Galaxy S21 Ultra device.

Pro Tip: To configure your S Pen settings, follow the path below to access the settings options

→ *Settings* > tap (Advanced features) > S Pen

About the Author

Edwin Brown is a tech reviewer and a professional forex trader. He is also a blog writer with Techmatrix.